T0163110

DEWEY IN 90 MINUTES

Dewey
IN 90 MINUTES

Paul Strathern

IVAN R. DEE
CHICAGO

DEWEY IN 90 MINUTES. Copyright © 2002 by Paul
Strathern. All rights reserved, including the right to reproduce
this book or portions thereof in any form. For information,
address: Ivan R. Dee, Publisher, 1332 North Halsted Street,
Chicago 60622. Manufactured in the United States of America
and printed on acid-free paper.

Library of Congress Cataloging-in-Publication Data:
Strathern, Paul, 1940–
    Dewey in 90 minutes / Paul Strathern.
      p. cm.
    Includes bibliographical references and index.
    ISBN 1-56663-476-8 (alk. paper) — ISBN 1-56663-475-X
(pbk. : alk. paper)
    1. Dewey, John, 1859–1952. I. Title: Dewey in ninety
minutes. II. Title.

B945.D44 S77 2002
191—dc21   2002073675

Contents

DEWEY IN 90 MINUTES

Dewey's Life and Works

During the first half of the twentieth century, John Dewey was regarded in America as the foremost philosopher of his age. This was no mean feat at a time when Bertrand Russell, Wittgenstein, and Heidegger were all alive and producing some of their finest work. Russell himself called Dewey "the leading living philosopher of America." The fact that Dewey had once saved Russell's life should not be seen as influencing this view. Both men took philosophy far too seriously to let any such indebtedness influence their opinions. Russell also described Dewey as "a man of the highest character, liberal in outlook, generous and kind in personal relations, indefatigable in work." But this did not stop him from regarding Dewey's pragmatic view of truth as nothing less than a philosophic catastrophe, liable to lead to lunacy. In Russell's view: "The concept of 'truth' as something dependent upon facts largely outside human control has been one of the ways in which philosophy hitherto has inculcated the necessary element of humility. When this check upon pride is removed, a further step is taken on the road towards a certain kind of madness."

John Dewey was born October 20, 1859, close to the Canadian border in Vermont. The states of Texas, California, and Florida had only recently been admitted to the Union; the internal combustion engine would not be invented until the following year; and there were the first rumblings of a civil war between the Northern and Southern states. The Dewey family had been Vermont farmers for three generations, and Dewey's father, Archibald, ran a local grocery business in Burlington, which was then a small but thriving lumber city on the banks of Lake Champlain. His mother, Lucinda, came from a well-known local political family—John's great-grandfather had been a Washington congressman for ten years.

John Dewey's early childhood was disturbed by the Civil War, which broke out when he was just a year old. Although Archibald Dewey was already forty, he immediately responded to Lincoln's call for volunteers and enlisted as a quartermaster in the 1st Vermont Cavalry. When he was sent south, Lucinda took the family to Virginia so that they could remain together, and they did not return to Burlington until the Civil War ended. By now Burlington was in the process of becoming the second largest lumber depot in the country. Amidst the atmosphere of booming business, the middle classes (which included the Deweys) lived in conditions of some prosperity. Meanwhile, down by the lakeside, squalid tenements housed the poor immigrant workers, who were mainly Irish and French Canadian. These slums were described in a contemporary local report as "abodes of wretchedness and filth" which had become "haunts of dissipation." Unlike many of the well-to-do families, the Deweys did not remain indifferent to such social injustice, and Lucinda Dewey undertook philanthropic work. As a result, though her son John was brought up and educated amidst "old American" culture, he was constantly aware of what life was like on the other side of the tracks.

Young John had an evangelical Christian schooling, which left a marked influence on his character and outlook. For years to come he would believe that redemption meant "to be delivered from the dominating lower life of the flesh, to be rescued to the higher life of the spirit, and to be shaped into a spiritual manhood." He would remain a practicing Christian throughout his long life. The moral and compassionate outlook he received from his faith would color not only his philosophical but also his social views.

After showing academic promise in high school, Dewey went on to study at the University of Vermont, where students who frequented the local billiard parlors and other "objectionable places of resort" were open to expulsion. But as is often the case with university authorities, such public strictures were little more than a vain attempt to curb the usual student behavior. The University of Vermont was no more or less rowdy than similar institutions at the time, and John Dewey is listed as having taken part in his fair share of student misdemeanors (helping imprison a hapless instructor in his classroom, repeatedly failing to turn up for military drill, and so on).

Dewey graduated in 1879 and took up a teaching post at a high school in Oil City, Pennsylvania. By now the Pennsylvania oil boom was at its height. In Oil City and the surrounding countryside, "derricks peered up behind the houses, thronged the marshy flats, congregated on the slopes, climbed the precipitous bluffs and clung to the rocky ledges." Dewey remained a schoolteacher for three years. His inexperience and "old American" manners prevented him from being a successful teacher. One of his pupils later recalled "how terribly the boys behaved, and how long and fervent was the prayer with which he opened each school day." But it was during this time that Dewey's interest in philosophy began to deepen. 1877 had seen the bicentenary of Spinoza's death, and the result had been a revival of interest in his philosophy, with a succession of articles discussing his ideas appearing in magazines over the next few years. Dewey began reading Spinoza, finding solace in the spirituality and geometrical abstraction of his philosophical method. On the other hand, he was unable to accept Spinoza's pantheism, which saw the world as God, and God as the world. In Dewey's view, this simply did not take account of the world as we lived in it. Experience in general, and doubtless classroom experience in particular, had taught Dewey that the world around us is not entirely divine. He wrote an article setting out his criticism and sent it to the *Journal of Speculative Philosophy*, where it was eventually published.

Encouraged by this turn of events, Dewey borrowed $500 from an aunt and registered for advanced study in philosophy at the Johns Hopkins University in Baltimore. At the time, the research and graduate program there was considered the finest in the land, the only one in America to match those at the leading European universities such as Cambridge, the Sorbonne, and Heidelberg. While studying at Hopkins, Dewey fell under the influence of Sylvester Morris, a professor of philosophy who was a leading neo-Hegelian. In later life Dewey still remembered Morris being possessed of "an ardor for ideas which amounted to spiritual fervor." Dewey quickly became converted to Morris's neo-Hegelian ideas. To this point he had found himself troubled by the many dualities he had encountered in life: the contrast between his comfortable upbringing and the shanty slums of Burlington, the spirituality he professed in church and the natural exhuberances of young manhood, his own well-intentioned kindliness and the indiscipline of his pupils. Neo-Hegelianism showed him a way to overcome these difficulties.

The German philosopher Georg Wilhelm Friedrich Hegel died in 1831, but the influence of his systematic idealistic philosophy had continued to be all-pervasive. His thought had been advanced and developed by thinkers across the entire spectrum, from Karl Marx to right-wing

Prussian bureaucrats. Basically Hegel had taught that the world operated according to a dialectical dynamic, which linked the minutest particulars to the loftiest and most abstract ideas in a vast, all-embracing system. Within this dialectic each thesis generated its own antithesis, a conflict that then became resolved in a synthesis of the two—which in turn became another thesis, and so on. For instance, the concept "being" generated its opposite "nonbeing," and these two conflicting notions then became synthesized into "becoming." This dynamic operated throughout all things, all ideas—the entire universe. Hegel's emphasis on the organic wholeness of the world enabled Dewey to reconcile the conflicts he had encountered, and he embraced neo-Hegelianism with all the fervor of his mentor Morris.

The other leading philosopher whose ideas touched Dewey during these years was Charles S. Peirce, who was also teaching at Johns Hopkins. Peirce's theory of scientific logic laid the foundations for pragmatism, the philosophy that Dewey would later develop, bringing him worldwide renown. Curiously, Dewey found Peirce's lectures a deep disappointment. As he wrote informally to a friend: "I think Mr. Peirce don't think [sic] there is any Phil. outside the generalizations of physical science." This surmise was correct, but the twenty-two-year-old Dewey was not ready for such modern ideas. He thought Peirce's lectures "appeal more strongly to the mathematical students than to the philosophical." Astonishingly, it would take Dewey almost twenty years to accept what Peirce had taught him. The memory of Peirce's ideas was to remain with him, for the most part unconsciously. When finally understood and accepted, they would prove seminal.

Charles S. Peirce was in many ways a remarkable man, though Dewey was far from being alone in not immediately recognizing this. No less an authority than the Encyclopedia Britannica now describes Peirce as the "most original and versatile intellect the Americas have so far produced." Some claim. And it has some justification. Peirce's role in establishing the philosophy of pragmatism would have been enough to make him a major figure. His influence on Dewey—and the definition of terms he bequeathed to Dewey—would likewise have secured him a leading place in American intellectual history. But this is only half the story. Peirce refused to be limited; his influence extended far beyond philosophy. Psychology, engineering, chemistry, astronomy, surveying, physics, mathematics, the "evolving theory of reality," and logic—especially logic—were all fields where Peirce made original, often highly significant contributions.

Needless to say, no university in such a conservative era was willing to accept such a free-ranging intellectual on a permanent basis. Peirce did at one stage entertain hopes of being appointed to a chair of logic research, but no such post yet existed, and no enterprising seat of learning was willing to risk establishing one for him. His four years as a lecturer at Johns Hopkins would prove his longest appointment. Among his students, Dewey's attitude would prove typical: the philosophers thought him best suited to mathematics and science studies; the scientists simply weren't interested in philosophy.

Meanwhile in Europe, where great scientific advances were being made, the scientists were heatedly debating the philosophical implications of the latest scientific discoveries; and the philosophers were becoming increasingly involved in scientific debate for the same reasons. Just a few examples will suffice to show the importance of this development. During the next decades Einstein would study Spinoza and Hume, whose ideas would greatly assist him in the concept of relativity. The philosophers Russell and Whitehead would attempt to establish the logical foundations of mathematics. Meanwhile the Austrian scientist-philosopher Ernst Mach (after whom the speed of sound is named) would argue strongly against the existence of the atom on empirical grounds: "No experiment has ever produced evidence of an atom." Such philosophical-scientific cross-fertilization would play a leading role in the major discoveries of the next half-century. As a direct result of such interests, evidence for the existence of atoms would be produced, relativity would be discovered, and the incompleteness of mathematics would be proved. The importance of the overlap between science and philosophy during this period is almost impossible to exaggerate. Peirce and his friend the psychologist and philosopher William James were among the first in America to understand the implications of this development.

At the age of fifty-two, Peirce retired to a remote farm on the Delaware River in Pennsylvania, where he lived in near destitution for the remaining twenty-three years of his life. He referred to himself as a "bucolic logician" and would not have survived but for the generosity of William James, who recognized Peirce for the universal genius he was. (Among Peirce's lesser achievements during this period was a pioneer design for an electric circuit-switching prototype computer, which can be found sketched out in one of his letters.) Two centuries earlier, when Newton had been asked how he had managed to make such great mathematical and scientific discoveries, he had modestly replied: "by standing on the shoulders of giants." Peirce was the philosophical giant on whose shoulders Dewey would one day stand.

But all this lay far in the future. Dewey proved to be a slow developer: his originality only gradually emerged in all its multifaceted intellectual form. In 1894 Dewey left Johns Hopkins with his Ph.D. and became an instructor in philosophy and psychology at the University of Michigan. There he further developed his neo-Hegelian ideas while at the same time pursuing his own research in the very latest experimental psychology. (This subject had been founded as a separate field of study only a decade or so earlier in Leipzig by the German "father of experimental psychology," Wilhelm Wundt.)

It was around this time that Dewey met Alice Chipman, who had been a village schoolteacher before coming to study at the University of Michigan. They both shared a passionate interest in philosophy, and Alice's outlook on the subject soon began to influence Dewey. Her belief that philosophy should apply itself to the real problems that beset real people in the everyday world shook Dewey out of his more academic approach to the classic problems studied throughout the long history of philosophy. But it proved to be only the beginning of a long process for Dewey, who still clung to his belief in neo-Hegelianism. John Dewey and Alice Chipman were married as soon as she graduated in 1886, and a year later they had a son.

In the same year Dewey published his first book, *Psychology*, which amazingly sought to reconcile the laboratory work of his experimental psychology with the out-and-out metaphysical philosophy of his neo-Hegelianism. His former professor of psychology at Johns Hopkins marveled at this ambitious intellectual endeavor: "That the absolute idealism of Hegel could be so cleverly adapted to be 'read into' such a range of facts, new and old, is indeed a surprise as great as when geology and zoology are ingeniously subjected to the rubrics of the six days of creation." The book soon became a center of academic controversy, with even Dewey's students taking sides in the argument. The student magazine at Michigan was somewhat more robust than Dewey's former psychology professor:

Having one foot in heaven, the other on earth

And in lieu of real seeing, his fancy gives birth

To wild speculations, as solid and fair

As water on quicksand, or smoke in the air.

Partly as a result of his wife's influence, Dewey now began to develop an interest in educational theory. His own bitter experiences in the blackboard jungle had convinced him that all was not right with education in America. As ever, when failed teachers write on this subject it is never the teachers who are to blame. The entire system was wrong. Yet Dewey's burgeoning originality was soon beginning to show here too. He saw that in sticking to traditional methods, schools were ignoring the experimental discoveries that were now being made in the new field of child psychology. Also, schools were simply not attuned to the social changes taking place in the emergent democracy of postbellum America. He

21

saw a need for an entirely new philosophy of education.

In 1894, after ten years at Michigan, Dewey was appointed to a professorship at the University of Chicago. This university had been founded just three years earlier with lavish funds provided by John D. Rockefeller. Its president, William Rainey Harper, was already establishing Chicago as one of the leading centers for research and advanced study in the country, and Dewey was appointed to head the newly created department of philosophy, psychology, and pedagogy—an assignment that could not have suited his skills better. (Ironically, Peirce had earlier been considered for the post, but his pragmatic ideas had been regarded as too unorthodox.) It was here that Dewey would thrive and make his name as an original pragmatic philosopher, psychologist, and educator.

Dewey's experimental work now led him to a growing understanding of the all-pervasive effect of Darwin's theory of evolution. The implications of Darwinism in psychology, philosophy, and even education became clear. Life appeared to evolve by means of a struggle in which the fittest survived, rather than by a process of dialectical unfolding. Yet for his first few years at Chicago Dewey still retained his belief in "experimental idealism"—the intellectual balancing act that managed to reconcile his neo-Hegelian metaphysics with the material of his experimental work. But it was becoming clear to him that this increasingly schizophrenic position was untenable. The dualisms that Dewey had so longed to resolve were once again catching up with him.

Did Hegel's dialectical process in fact mirror the rational workings of the real world? It all came down to logic. Hegel had believed that "our logical processes are simply the reading off or coming to consciousness of the inherently rational structure already possessed by the universe in virtue of the presence within it of this pervasive and constitutive action of thought." But this view of logic made no allowance for genuine scientific activity as pursued by scientists. There was no room for skepticism and questioning—doubt and experimental inquiry had no place in such an all-inclusive metaphysical scheme of things. Dewey came to realize that what was required was a logic where "all the distinctions and terms of thought—judgment, concept, inference, subject, predicate . . . etc. . . . shall be interpreted simply and entirely as distinctive functions or divisions of labor within the doubt-inquiry process." The main object of logic should be to explain "the eternal nature of thought and its eternal validity in relation to an eternal reality."

It was time to abandon the old unanswerable conundrums of classical philosophy. Is the world logical, or is this just our way of looking at the world? What is truth? Does our thought match reality? Such questions should simply be dismissed. We must forget the idea that there is such a thing as "thought in general," which attempts to find the true picture of "reality in general." Instead we should concentrate on the particular problem at hand. Thought is not general, it is specific. It deals with real problems which arise in our particular personal experience.

Dewey's logic was to be an "instrumental

type of logic." It was like the process involved in a single laboratory experiment. It was a plan of action intended to solve a particular practical problem. The truth of instrumental logic had nothing to do with how it did (or did not) match some notional reality. This was irrelevant. What mattered was "its functional or instrumental use in affecting the transition from a relatively conflicting experience to a relatively integrated one." Its use was to solve problems, to resolve conflicts.

This insistence upon the particular, and its relation to the personal, would become the characteristic of Dewey's philosophy. From now on this would be the method Dewey would use to resolve the dualities that so disturbed him. Here he managed to relate the experimental to the personal—both for himself and as a universally applicable method. Logic was what worked. Hence the name "pragmatism," which became attached to his philosophy. (Dewey was not happy with this name, preferring to call his philosophy "instrumentalism" or "experimentalism." These do in fact better describe what he was doing, yet pragmatism captures the kernel of his idea.) The word "pragmatic" comes from the ancient Greek word meaning active, businesslike, versed in affairs, relating to matter of fact. It has connotations of public activity and function. Pragmatism was like science: you used it, and it worked. If it didn't work, you discarded it.

Pragmatism was essentially a scientific view of the world. As such, its tendency was to be down-to-earth and commonsensical. The ultimate reality was nothing more or less than the reality we encounter in everyday life. The nature that is subjected to scientific experiments, the reality we wake up to in the morning—there was no ultimate mystery here.

Such a view very much coincides with the state of science in the last decades of the nineteenth century. Experimental science had made huge advances which were already beginning to bear technological fruit. But the theoretical underpinning of science—its basic laws and substance—seemed to have been all but established. In the scientific community it was widely believed that the golden years of theoretical scientific discovery were almost certainly coming to an end. Around this time the young Max Planck was being advised against taking up theoretical physics because "it would soon be finished." The main discoveries had already been made. All that remained was mopping up—the long painstaking process of experimentation. Chemistry too appeared to be in a similar state. The Russian chemist Mendeleyev had drawn up his Periodic Table, which listed all known and knowable elements along with their weights and properties. The Austrian physicist Boltzmann was convinced that these elements were constituted of ultimate particles in the form of atoms. There just didn't seem to be room for any more great discoveries concerning the ultimate physical nature of the world we inhabited. From now on, science would simply consist of experiments.

The first evidences undermining this view were not recognized as such. When Madame Curie discovered radioactivity in the 1890s, it was regarded by many as just another chemical property. The idea that atoms might disintegrate was unthinkable. When, in 1900, Planck noted the quantum effect—whereby light appeared to be both a particle *and* a wave—it was widely assumed to be just a tiresome anomaly, which would soon be explained away. An observable phenomenon was either an effect or an object, it could not be both. Then the entire structure came tumbling down: Einstein's theory of relativity destroyed the absolute certainties of space and time. It became understood that Madame Curie had discovered something distinct from atoms and their chemical properties. Finally, it was accepted that quantum theory was here to stay. The certainties of the late-nineteenth-century scientific world were destroyed forever: an entirely new theoretical picture was beginning to emerge.

Amazingly, pragmatism would survive this revolution. Science itself would completely change, but this would not destroy or even undermine Dewey's scientific philosophy. Dewey had always insisted upon the particular and its relation to the personal. He saw his instrumental logic purely as a method of treating disturbing problems and bringing them to a state of personally satisfying resolution. Such logic provided the link between the individual and the reality he inhabited, between the psychological and the scientific. It joined the fluidities of the personal to the rigidities of the material world (as it was then seen). Here both contingency and necessity could exist side by side. This approach dissolved yet another of the great befuddling mysteries that had for so long beset classical philosophy. How can we be free in a logically necessary world? How can the free will we are convinced we experience in fact exist in a predetermined scientific universe? For Dewey, all this was a pseudo-problem. The arguments for free will and determinism, which had for so long beset philosophy, were simply circumvented by his instrumental logic. It alone showed how we could be free and still be scientific beings in a scientific world. When we applied ourselves to the resolution of specific scientific problems, the problem of free will versus determinism simply vanished.

This ability to cope with uncertainty enabled Dewey's essentially scientific philosophy to survive the great transformation of science that occurred at the close of the nineteenth century. Dewey could not have foreseen this transformation; no one did. For once, not even the ancient Greeks had suspected that the world was anything like this. Democritus had come up with the idea of atoms. Others had suggested that the universe might be almost infinitely vast. But no one—no scientist or thinker over the intervening millennia—had come remotely close to suspecting the existence of quantum reality. Indeed, it is said that Aristotle could have understood Newton and Darwin, and might well have been able to grasp all the great scientific discoveries to the end of the nineteenth century. It has been suggested that he might even have understood relativity if he had been able to talk it over with Einstein. Such a thing could *possibly* have been foreseen, once the full extent of the universe was understood. But quantum theory Aristotle would not have been able to understand or even foresee. He would never have been able to conceive of anything like it. And why not? Because it is quite simply inconceivable. As the great American quantum physicist Richard Feynman put it: "Anyone who claims he understands quantum physics doesn't know what he's talking about." Here, among the foundations of matter, exists a phenomenon which appears to resist overall comprehension by the human mind. We can observe some of its effects, we can even attempt to measure some of them (but not all of them, not at the same time), but we cannot claim to understand it. Here was a phenomenon that defeated logic. Yet it did not defeat instrumental logic, which could in many ways have been designed specifically to deal with such a thing. Dewey's pragmatism regarded the experimental results of the particular instance as sacred. There could be no question of contradiction *at this level*. What was observed was observed: how we used this was the truth—there was no universal truth "out there" waiting to be discovered.

The scientific revolution that took place after the turn of the twentieth century meant that science would never be the same again. Essentially it was the ultimate *certainty* of science that was destroyed. The mechanical world, with everything in it being utterly predestined, was gone

31

forever. The universe did not run like clockwork. But as we have seen, Dewey's scientific world-view was never utterly predictable. There was no necessity about his logic; it was functional. Dewey's ideas were, if anything, strengthened by the introduction of such things as quantum indeterminacy. The Newtonian mechanical world had operated according to fixed laws. As Dewey put it, a world without contingency, one that was totally predetermined and fixed in its course, would exist as "only a block universe, either something ended and admitting of no change, or else a predestined march of events." But a world in which apparent necessity and contingency coexisted was a changing world whose outcome was not predictable. As he put it: "We live in a world which is an impressive and irresistible mixture of sufficiencies, tight completeness, order, recurrences which make possible prediction and control, and singularities, ambiguities, uncertain possibilities, processes going on to consequences as yet indeterminate."

During the course of the twentieth century science itself would be forced to accept such a state of affairs. The uncertainties of quantum physics and relativity—the micro and the macro worlds—permeated the entire scientific world. Laws were no longer taken to be fixed and immutable, as if carved in stone for all eternity. Instead of being exact descriptions of natural objects, processes, and structures, they tended to be regarded as statistical averages. No scientific law was any longer said to be absolutely certain, just more or less highly probable. Probability replaced certainty. And for Dewey, where the personal and the scientific were one in specific events, "No mechanically exact science of an individual is possible. An individual is a history unique in character."

But this was just the beginning. Dewey's method of scientific inquiry could be extended well beyond the realms of science. In his view, the experimental method was also the most fruitful approach to ethical and social problems. Philosophy was practical or it was nothing. It was about human activity and should thus involve itself in human activity. Pursuing his attack on the uselessness of classical philosophy, he claimed that all knowledge is practical. Again and again he stressed how much his instrumentalism sought to make philosophy scientific. Classical philosophy had failed to explain the world we lived in or the life we lived in it. If anything, it had only made matters worse. In attempting to analyze our common experience it had simply made it incomprehensible. Where previously there had been no difficulty, philosophy had created insoluble dualities such as free will versus determinism, appearance versus reality, mind versus body. The scientific approach to reality, on the other hand, produced results of great consequence. Scientists did not concern themselves with the problem of whether they had in fact discovered anything *at all*. They didn't ask what knowledge was, they produced it. Likewise, they didn't stop to ask themselves whether the entire scientific enterprise was of any consequence. Their practical lives were already too deeply involved in it.

When this approach was applied to moral problems, it didn't get bogged down in utterly unanswerable questions about the ultimate nature of good. Dewey maintained there was no such thing as a final and timeless moral law which derived from the essential nature of humanity. Such irrelevant ideas were again circumvented when morality became a matter of a single person dealing with a specific problem in a particular circumstance. Morality should be concerned with the particular aspirations and concerns of real people in the real world, not abstractions in an abstract world.

Dewey went even further, specifically linking his instrumental way of thinking to the growth of democracy in America. He saw his moral attitude as the philosophical justification for liberal democracy. And for Dewey the concept of democracy was more than just the notion of a method of government: the rule of the people, by the people, for the people. A liberal democracy enabled its members to have the freedom to associate with one another and develop their lives experimentally. This gave them the opportunity to grow as human beings, to enlarge their experience and realize their full potential as individuals.

All this only further illustrated how classical philosophy had sidetracked itself. Where instrumentalism (or pragmatism) examined the practical foundations and consequences of its outlook, classical philosophy remained bewitched by its own tradition. It continued to be puzzled by its own self-imposed conundrums, simply because it refused to examine where they came from and the assumptions on which they were based. Dewey insisted upon attacking such assumptions, disregarding those premises that led only to insoluble conclusions. There was no place for such needless enigmas in a genuine practical and functional philosophy.

Dewey's attitude toward the classical mind-body problem was typical. Classical philosophers persisted in asking the unanswerable question: how could the immaterial mind have an effect on the material substance of the body? Dewey simply attacked the assumption underlying this question—the notion of material substance. Dewey insisted that "life, feeling, and thought are never independent of physical events." Likewise: "*Matter* has a definite assignable meaning in physical science. It designates something capable of being expressed in mathematical symbols." But "it is not possible to generalize the definite meaning 'matter' has in this context of physical science into a philosophical view." He goes on to stress: "*If* the term 'matter' is given a philosophical interpretation, over and above its technical scientific meaning—e.g., *mass* until recently—this meaning, I believe, should be to name a *functional* relation rather than a substance." To ask how immaterial "mind" can affect material "body" (or matter, or substance) thus becomes redundant. Dewey's functionalism fully accounts for this relation. It explains away any "mind-body" problem by reducing any problem to the actual circumstances in which it takes place, and what is observed to happen.

Dewey's rejection of dualities, and his search for ways of overcoming their difficulties, remains a curious echo of his earlier neo-Hegelian dialectic. But instead of subjecting such problems to a metaphysical resolution, he insisted upon discovering a functional scientific answer. This would be applied to an entire range of popularly recognized dualities. Dewey insisted that, when viewed in the light of specific function, there was no distinction between such things as man and nature, the individual and society, the organism and the environment, thought and action, means and ends, or even fact and value. Ethics, psychology, sociology, biology, politics— all could be approached, their problems solved, by means of his instrumentalism. It pointed to a seamless continuity between all human knowledge.

Even logic became one with the subject in which it was involved. Dewey saw logic as a theory of inquiry. For him it was not an abstract or formal method so much as a general account of how human thought functions. It was inseparable from the problems it set out to solve, whether these were in science or everyday life. His personal need to resolve dualities gave this logic a psychological dimension. The logic of his instrumentalism was seen as an inquiry which sought to resolve a disturbing situation into a pleasing solution. What was required was intelligent, and as far as possible informed, investigation of the problem at hand. Basically the same method applied in the laboratory as in government.

Essential to this view of knowledge was Dewey's notion of "fallibilism." There was no certain knowledge, there were no eternal fixed principles or rules. Everything had to be tested to discover its fallibility. In this way knowledge progressed, in all fields. Here we come to the core of Dewey's theory of knowledge, which as we have seen reaches out into all realms of human endeavor. But what precisely *is* this method, this functional logic, this progressive way of knowing, this "inquiry" as he called it? In Dewey's words: "Inquiry is the controlled or directed transformation of an indeterminate situation into one that is so determinate in its constituent distinctions and relations as to convert the elements of the original situation into a unified whole." What precisely is he talking about? To discover the truth of this too will evidently require a certain amount of inquiry. What does he mean? In his own words: "Inquiry is concerned with objective transformations of objective subject-matter." It is "attempting to make the world more organic." Its result is not any abstract timeless "truth" but "organic wholes."

In the end, is this anything more than the empiricism of scientific method? Dewey himself admits "that my idea of experience and hence of empirical method is naturalistic." That is, it insists that all our experience is derived from the world of nature and nothing else. His emphasis is on the biological. "For many years I have . . . maintained that the key to a philosophical theory of experience must proceed from initially linking it with the processes and functions of life as the latter are disclosed in biological science." He goes on to explain: "The things of experience are produced . . . by interaction of organism and environing conditions." He also maintains that "the self, the 'subject' of action, is a factor *within* experience."

But Dewey's distrust of "truth" fails to overcome the problem of generalizing from particular empirical experience. This can be done only by induction: by inferring from a repetition of particular events to some general rule. According to induction, such general rules tend to be reinforced the more confirming instances we observe. For example, we observe that exposure to radioactivity above a certain level is always fatal—though we can never know for certain that our next experience will not disprove this rule. Indeed, the eighteenth-century Scottish philosopher Hume showed that even the strictest empirical induction is forced to rely upon the assumption of a metaphysical truth that we can never experience. That is, in order to accept induction we must first of all believe "that the future will resemble the past." It is impossible for any thoroughgoing empiricism to circumvent this. Dewey tended to dismiss the point, for the simple reason that science, our everyday experience, common sense, and so forth, all lead us to accept the continuity and consistency of our experience. This was just another of those pseudo-problems of classical philosophy that obfuscate our experience rather than clarify it. We simply have to believe in the future consistency of experience.

Dewey proposed that we have two types of

belief, "good" and "bad." They are not true or false—that we cannot know. Our ideas fall into one category or the other depending upon the effect they have upon us. If they lead us into fruitful activity, they are good. According to this progressive view of knowledge, ideas can also change category. Indeed, they are almost bound to do so. Ideas will be better than those they have replaced, but not as good as those that succeed them. There is no such thing as a simple static "true idea."

It was Bertrand Russell who pointed out the fatal flaw in this argument. In history we have ideas about what actually took place. According to Dewey, these will be good or bad depending upon the effect they have upon our behavior. Russell convincingly points out that most historians are more concerned with whether an event actually took place than the effect of this event upon our present behavior. He goes on to reduce Dewey's position to absurdity with the following example. I am asked: "Did you have coffee this morning?" Before making any reply I am likely to reflect upon the truth of my answer, rather than its effect. But even if I do choose the latter, *I cannot be sure what this will be.* I cannot test beforehand whether my answer is a "good" idea or a "bad" one. In dispensing altogether with the notion of truth in his progressive theory of knowledge, Dewey leaves us without a guide here. If we cannot test beforehand whether our ideas are good or bad, how are we to choose between them?

Similar objections can be made with regard to Dewey's moral theory. We may accept that there is no such thing as an ultimate, certain, and unquestionable moral good, but this does not mean that we judge everything by its "good" or "bad" effect. We are capable of choosing something we believe is right, even when we know its effects may be calamitous. There may be little room for selfless heroism or martyrdom amidst the pragmatism of the modern scientific world, but that does not mean we must absolve ourselves from any attempt to explain such things. The person who acts for a metaphysical good, and in so doing produces a catastrophic effect in the physical world, is not incomprehensible.

43

Even if we abhor his belief system, our philosophical system should seek to understand him. If it does not, it is deeply flawed—and its "effect" may be just as bad as the idea it opposes. Dewey may have been keen to resolve such opposing dualities, but this cannot be done by pragmatic (or intrumentalist) means as he proposed them.

Many, including Dewey himself, saw the above objections to pragmatic induction as none too damaging. The functionalism of science—and the scientific approach—progressed regardless of such niggling objections. These criticisms were dismissed as belonging to the past or the fainthearted. Science was here to stay; classical philosophy had had its day, and its enigmas were part of history. But a more serious flaw arose with regard to mathematics. The contemporary philosopher W. T. Jones goes so far as to claim: "One of the test cases for Dewey's whole analysis is the nature and status of mathematical thinking." Because mathematics is fundamental to the whole modern scientific outlook, much is at stake here for Dewey's scientific theory of

44

knowledge. The problem of mathematics and its status resembles yet another of the classical philosophical conundrums that Dewey so abhorred. Put simply: Does mathematics somehow exist independent of our thinking, or is it entirely "ours"? Dewey insisted upon the latter. Mathematical concepts are nothing more than conceptual implements which we use in action. They have no existence outside their function. Mathematics differs from our other functions only in its great precision.

The first and most obvious objection to this view is that mathematics does not have "great precision"—it has *exactitude*. To suggest that $2 + 2 = 2.00000001$ is an absurdity. It is also untrue (which suggests that there is such a thing as "truth" in our knowledge). Likewise, it will remain untrue no matter how our inductive knowledge progresses. Dewey does in fact go some way toward meeting this objection. He distinguishes between "operations overtly performed" and "operations *symbolically* executed." He recognizes that a "great step forward [in human history] was made when special symbols were derived that were emancipated from the load of irrelevancy carried by words developed for social rather than intellectual purposes." Such symbols were "framed in detachment from direct overt use and *with respect to one another.*" But Dewey points out that this leads to a fallacy. "Independence from any specified application is readily taken to be equivalent to independence from application as such." According to Dewey, this step is "the origin of that idolatrous attitude toward universals so often recurring in the history of human thought." People began to handle such universal ideas as if they were things.

Dewey now points out that the real distinction is between "operations to be actually performed and possible operations." The latter deal with "their logical relations *to one another.*" This "opens up opportunities for operations that would never be directly suggested." This is indeed how mathematics provides ingenious practical solutions. But Dewey goes on to assert that for such thinking, "its origins and eventual meaning lie in acts that deal with concrete situations." Yet, as he has already admitted, the manipulation of pure mathematics (abstract ideas, universals, numbers) "opens up opportunities for operations." However, many of these operations remain without application. Dewey finally claims: "The difficulties and paradoxes which have been found to attend the logic of numbers disappear when instead of their being treated as essences or as properties of things in existence, they are viewed as designations of potential operations." In other words, even the most abstruse of pure and inapplicable mathematics should not be regarded as an investigation of mathematical abstractions but as the formulation of possible applications. Math was essentially practical, or it was nothing. One day a use would be found for such apparent abstractions—which would then be seen to be a method of dealing with practical objects rather than the abstract manipulation of universal ideas.

It is worth comparing Dewey's argument with the complementary viewpoint posed by the contemporary French mathematical collective Bourbaki, which sought to answer why mathematics "fits" the world in such precise and astonishing fashion—and continues to do so as further, ever more intricate discoveries are made. According to Bourbaki, mathematics fits the world because it attempts to describe all possibilities, whereas the world inevitably consists only of some possibilities.

Dewey also claims that "mathematical space is not a kind of space distinct from so-called physical and empirical space." But it is. Mathematical space is infinitely divisible. Compare this with latest investigations of physics: these posit the existence of extremely minute superstrings as the ultimate (i.e., indivisible) entity. Furthermore, the ultimate reality of superstrings is said to involve eleven dimensions. Mathematical space, on the other hand, can accommodate an infinity of dimensions. Here Einstein's remark concerning the nature of mathematics is of particular relevance: "As far as the laws of mathematics refer to reality, they are not certain; and as far as they are certain, they do not refer to reality." The *certainty* of mathematics—perhaps its most characteristic feature—simply does not apply to reality, and never can.

The existence of such purely mathematical truth contradicts Dewey's functionalism, and this would seem seriously to undermine his entire scientific theory of knowledge. We may live in the age of science, but this does not mean that science as we know it will last forever as the paradigm of how we acquire knowledge. Even to suggest that from now on every age will be scientific is to make unwarranted assumptions about human knowledge. For the time being, science may have everything to say while traditional philosophy has precious little to say. Yet philosophy as such will always remain deeper than science. Why? Because it attempts to examine the roots of knowledge, the assumptions upon which knowledge rests, what it actually achieves, and so forth. Science is only the contents. When philosophy asks whether in fact science has discovered anything at all in the way of certain knowledge, it holds itself up to commonsense scorn. But such questions must continue to be asked. Like the opposition party in a democracy, philosophy has an essential role to play here. History has witnessed entire landscapes of human knowledge subsiding into the sea of skepticism. Such knowledges as sorcery, astrology, and astronomy were all accepted as central to human identity in their time. More recently, the "death of God" has led humanity to scrutinize and question the entire Western spiritual tradition. And this wealth of knowledge has far exceeded the importance of scientific thought through most of the formative millennia of civilized Western humanity's development. Much of this spiritual knowledge is now largely absorbed or abandoned. If history is anything to go by, science too must undergo this process. It must always expect to arouse philosophic skepticism. The scientific endeavor has certainly transformed humanity, allowing it to develop its potential as never before. Dewey was right in seeing this and in seeking to encourage this tendency. At the same time, science has also given rise to unprecedented dangers. The scientific endeavor could easily have put an end to our species during the years of "nuclear deterrence." And it might yet render the planet uninhabitable by human beings. Under such circumstances, the progressive scientific functionalism espoused by Dewey cannot simply be regarded as the modern version of the truth. It too must overcome the "unproductive" objections posed by classical philosophy. Dewey simply regarded these as unanswerable pseudo-problems—others in the twentieth century would regard them as linguistic errors, chimeras, or unnecessary, self-inflicted "mysteries." The science-inspired philosophies of the twentieth century tended to concur that "There is no riddle." But the fact that such questions have persisted—despite their apparent unanswerabilty—speaks volumes. There appears to be an unfulfilled human need which prompts us to confront the traditional conundrums of philosophy, to ask these unanswerable questions. And this need is not assuaged by sleight-of-hand sophistry which attempts to persuade it that such questions simply don't exist.

As we have seen, Dewey's thought was deeply concerned with practical application. In line with this, his philosophical thought played a leading part in his psychological and educational theory. All of these made great advances during his years at the University of Chicago. Our psychological behavior and our learning processes were characterized as a process of inquiry. Doubt and uncertainty prompted us to attempt a resolution of these difficulties. Stress sought relief, conflict sought remedy, ignorance sought knowledge. This was especially true in education, which Dewey was convinced must begin with, and be grounded in, experience. Education is not simply a matter of arid learning; it should instead be a process of enlightening enquiry.

Such liberal ideas sound all very well in theory. But Dewey insisted upon them being put into practice. As part of his department he opened a Laboratory School at the University of Chicago, which exists to this day. (Its rather ominous technical name soon became replaced in popular usage by "The Dewey School.") Here Dewey's ideas were developed into practical educational methods. Relating the child's psychology to his or her experience was the key. Our psychology was crucial to the way we learned. This should not be an arduous and passive process but an active project of inquiry. The teacher should encourage the child to embark upon this journey of inquiry with enthusiasm. In childhood we are confronted with a world we do not understand. Education should lead us through the psychological process of coming to terms with this world. In childhood, at the outset of the educational experience, how did we react to a world that we did not understand? The teacher should understand this psychological situation of the children, helping them to overcome the doubt and uncertainty induced by their initial experience of the strange and inexplicable aspects of the world. In order to do this, teachers must gain the trust of their children. They should not command their pupils but interact with them. The traditional approach of discipline and rote learning only stifled the child's need to inquire. The teacher should be regarded as a fellow traveler along the road to knowledge: a guide, rather than a taskmaster. In this way pupils would learn how to achieve all aspects of their potential as human beings. A holistic attitude toward growth was encouraged.

Dewey's educational philosophy was to cause a small revolution in American teaching methods. His effect might have been even greater but for the somewhat overenthusiastic application of his ideas by some of his unsupervised followers. The results of overliberalization in the classroom would in time cause a predictable backlash. Nonetheless his ideas would eventually be absorbed throughout the educational system. His principles for democratic teaching were in tune with the new democratic age.

But it was not always easy. Dewey's ideas eventually brought him into conflict with local authorities. These problems came to a head when one of the city's schools was merged with Dewey's school, and he appointed his wife as headmistress. There followed a series of misunderstandings with the university president, William Rainey Harper, and in 1904 Dewey resigned.

Such was Dewey's renown that he was soon offered a specially created chair in philosophy at

Columbia University in New York. He remained at Columbia for the rest of his career and became emeritus professor when he retired. During his forty-seven-year attachment to Columbia, he played an increasingly prominent role in public life. He provided an incisive analysis of public events and questions of the day with his regular contributions to the *New Republic* and other progressive journals. He continued to publish a stream of influential works in philosophy, psychology, and education. And he traveled widely, being an accredited intellectual celebrity wherever he went.

In 1919 Dewey and his wife visited Japan. Here he gave a series of public lectures at the Imperial University. The stated aim of these lectures, somewhat forbidding, was "to set forth the forces which make intellectual reconstruction inevitable and to prefigure some of the lines upon which it must proceed." The lectures evidently lived up to their promise. He started with an audience of almost a thousand. "They are a patient race," he wrote optimistically in a letter home. Within a few lectures his audience had dwindled to an extremely patient thirty. Despite its political advance into the modern world, Japan remained strictly conservative. The emperor was regarded as a god, and this theology permeated an education system where Dewey's ideas were greeted with incomprehension. Teachers in the public schools were the most zealous believers in the emperor cult, and Dewey noted that "more than one has been burned or allowed the children to be burned while he rescued the portrait of the emperor when there was a fire." Such action would result in an appearance at court, rather than in the courts. Meanwhile Mrs. Dewey attempted to promote the cause of women's suffrage—to equal incomprehension.

Next Dewey spent a year in China, where he lectured at the National University in Peking on philosophical topics ranging from the ancient Greeks to Bertrand Russell. Halfway through the year Russell himself arrived to lecture on his own philosophy. He was accompanied by his new mistress Dora Black, a social solecism that outraged the international diplomatic community. Dewey and his wife were the only ones willing to receive Russell and his partner in their house. When Russell fell ill, Dewey looked after him. Russell's health was soon so precarious that the local press jumped the gun and reported his death. As the news spread around the world, with obituaries appearing in the British and American press, Dewey and Russell were busy discussing philosophy. According to one report, Dewey was deeply moved by "the passion, sense of fun, and restless intelligence radiating from Russell on his presumed death-bed."

In 1928, at the age sixty-nine, Dewey was invited to visit the Soviet Union to see how education was progressing as a result of the Communist revolution. On arrival in Leningrad, he found himself immediately impressed by the will of the working people to educate themselves. He was also struck by the way the school curriculum emphasized the role of work in adult life. This was a realistic lesson that should be learned in any education system. He noted how pupils were encouraged to "act cooperatively and collectively as readily as now in capitalistic countries they act 'individualistically.'" On the other hand, he abhorred the extent of propaganda that appeared in the classroom. And despite his positive impressions, he was well aware that the secret police were always hovering in the background during his visit. He was not naive.

Later he reported on his visit in a series of articles for the *New Republic*. In these he suggested that the best way to regard events in the Soviet Union was as a social experiment on a national scale, one whose outcome no one could yet foresee. As with any experiment, there were always difficulties. But in this case the difficulties involved human beings, which meant that the experiment must proceed with extreme care. He candidly admitted that "for selfish reasons I prefer seeing it tried out in Russia rather than my own country."

As a result of Dewey's unprejudiced and evenhanded reports on the new Soviet state, he found himself regarded as "a propagandist for Communist interests." For the rest of his life he would be dogged by the suspicion, in some quarters, that he was a Communist. Anyone who had paid even the slightest attention to his liberal philosophy, his open-minded ideas on psychology, and his intensely nondidactic educational theories could have seen that this was sheer nonsense. Dewey's entire thinking was based on the democratic ideal.

Dewey landed himself in further political controversy in 1937 when he headed a commission to question Leon Trotsky, the Communist leader who had been exiled from Stalin's Russia and was now living in Mexico. The aim of the commission was to discover what precisely was going on in Russia. Stalin had been in power for fifteen years, and his rule was becoming increasingly dictatorial. He had recently ordered a series of "show trials" in Moscow. There senior Communist figures, many of whom had played a heroic role in the 1917 revolution, were tried on trumped-up charges of treason, brainwashed into confessing their "crimes," and then summarily shot. The civilized world had watched in horror. Russia's borders were as good as sealed, and it was felt that Trotsky, who had been Stalin's closest henchman before he had fled, might be able to shed light on what was actually happening. With this in mind, Dewey's commission set out for Mexico City in March 1937.

Dewey's venture incurred the wrath of both the extreme right and the extreme left. The Communists, in both the United States and Mexico, were strongly against what they saw as this recognition of the deviationist Trotsky and his attempt to discredit the Russian Revolution. The extreme right simply accused Dewey of having further dealings with Communists. As a result, Dewey's commission was subjected to considerable abuse and threats even before it reached Mexico. Dewey was by now seventy-eight years old, and many feared that the trip might affect his health. There was also the threat of possible assassination by Stalinist agents in Mexico.

The meetings with Trotsky were held in the villa of the celebrated Mexican mural painter Diego Rivera. Barricades were erected around the villa, manned by armed police. Inside, Dewey questioned Trotsky over a period of a week. According to one eyewitness report: "Once or twice, in instances where Trotsky's own statements clearly ran counter to Dewey's own democratic ideas, there was a scarcely noticeable change of tone. In these rare instances, Dewey's own independence of mind, in the face of Trotsky's brilliance, was apparent." (This is typical of reactions to Dewey throughout his life. His sheer decency, combined with his civilized, somewhat professorial bearing, caused many to underestimate him—regarding him as just another academic. Faced with Trotsky's "brilliance," Dewey showed himself to be quite his equal. A study of their respective works will show that if anything it is Trotsky's "brilliance" that time has found wanting.)

Dewey and his commission duly returned to the United States and issued their report. Dewey was in no doubt about the evidence passed on to him by Trotsky about Stalin and his "show trials." The state of the Russian Revolution illustrated one of Dewey's deepest philosophical tenets—his disbelief in the dualities of classical philosophy. In this case the pseudo-problem was the difference between means and ends. For Dewey there was no duality here, only an organic whole. As he put it: "The great lesson for all American radicals and for all sympathizers with the U.S.S.R. is that they must go back and reconsider the whole question of means of bringing about social changes and of truly democratic methods of approach to social progress. . . . The dictatorship of the proletariat has led and, I am convinced, always must lead to a dictatorship over the proletariat and over the party. I see no reason to believe that something similar would not happen in every country in which an attempt is made to establish a Communist government." These were prescient words in 1937—though Dewey's prescience did not extend to Trotsky's fate: three years later in Mexico City Stalin's former deputy was assassinated by Stalinist agents.

Dewey had retired from the Columbia faculty in 1930 but continued to play a prominent role in public affairs. He also continued his constant stream of books and articles. Among the leading works he produced during this period were *Logic, the Theory of Inquiry; Freedom and Culture;* and *Experience and Education.* The titles alone hint at the breadth of his reference.

Not the least of Dewey's achievements was his contribution to psychology. As always, this remained part and parcel of his philosophy, blending too with his educational and social principles. His study is always the *whole* of human nature, which he places in the midst of its involvements. For Dewey, psychology is function rather than detailed abstract theory. Not surprisingly, his psychology is firmly based upon social psychology. It involves three basic factors.

The first is habit, "in which the environment has its say as surely as the [organism]." Dewey distinguishes two types of habit: "intelligent and routine." A higher form of life will tend to "more complex, sure, and flexible" habits. Characteristically, he insisted upon the *functional* aspect of habit. It is intended to maintain and enrich life, assisting growth.

The second factor is impulse. Where habits are learned, impulses are the original source. Habits are how we learn to adapt to our impulses. In this way, though impulse initially gives rise to habit, it can in turn become shaped by habit. Impulses must therefore be capable of transformation. They do not have an unchanging character—as would be the case, for instance, in so-called blind impulse. They gain their meaning through their interaction with the social environment.

The third factor is intelligence. According to Dewey, this should be regarded as an entirely flexible form of habit, which is capable of altering and transforming other habits when they become restrictive rather than promoting further growth.

Explained briefly and theoretically in this fashion, Dewey's psychology inevitably appears somewhat barren. But it achieves its insight and fulfillment when it is applied: especially in an educational setting, or with regard to moral values. The stress is always on function and flexibility. For instance, as he explains: "Modern science, modern industry, and politics have presented us with an immense amount of material foreign to, often inconsistent with, the most prized intellectual and moral heritage of the Western world. This is the cause of our modern intellectual perplexities and confusions." The aim, as always, is the resolution of upsetting dualities and pseudo-problems: "the function of reflective thought is to transform a situation in which there is experienced obscurity, doubt, conflict, disturbance of some sort, into a situation that is clear, coherent, settled, harmonious." But avoidance of conflict *in itself* is not the aim. "The child learns to avoid the shock of unpleasant disagreement, to find the easy way out, to appear to conform to customs which are wholly mysterious to him in order to get his own way." This problem is not confined to childhood and education. "When we face this fact in its general significance, we confront one of the ominous aspects of the history of man." The aim, both of education and psychology, should be "intelligent guidance" toward growth and the realization of the full and holistic human potential. Once again, this may sound somewhat vague in words; the practice is another matter altogether.

Dewey's wife, Alice, had died in 1927 after several years of suffering from heart disease. Dewey remained a widower for almost two decades. At the age of eighty-seven, he married again, this time to Roberta Grant, whom he had known since childhood. He and his new wife continued to travel, and in the hot summer months he would leave New York for his cottage in Nova Scotia, off the east coast of Canada. His ninetieth birthday on October 20, 1949, was an international event. Dewey had already been recognized by the University of Paris as "the most profound, the most complete expression of American genius." Now it was the turn of presidents and premiers to pay their tribute. The leaders of more than fifteen countries, from all continents, sent personal greetings. Dewey replied by stating what his life had always been about. He had been "first, last, and all the time, engaged in the vocation of philosophy." But his aim had been to penetrate the surface of things and reach "a moderately clear and distinct idea of what the problems are that underlie the difficulties and evils which we experience *in fact*; that is to say, in *practical* life."

John Dewey died in 1952, at the age of ninety-two.

Afterword

When Dewey was born, Hegel still cast his shadow over European and American philosophy. By the time Dewey died, philosophy had seen the contributions of Schopenhauer, Nietzsche, Russell, Wittgenstein, Heidegger, and even Sartre. Despite the early influence of Hegel, Dewey produced a very American philosophy, essentially distinct from his great European contemporaries. His pragmatism (or instrumentalism, as he preferred to call it) was rooted in the practical. As such, it permeated all spheres of learning and activity. It was also very twentieth century. He saw science as the dominating form of knowledge. The methods of science he adapted to the methods of obtaining all knowledge. Experimentalism and experimental technique were what was needed to discover and test our new forms of knowledge. He rightly foresaw that the ever-changing twentieth century would require ever new ways of doing things, of learning things, of seeing things for what they were.

The twentieth century was also very much the "American century," when the United States rose from provincial power to world leadership. The character and attitude that sowed the seeds for such leadership were very much a part of the early-twentieth-century American ethos. This was the time of raw commercial enterprise and widespread European immigration. Pragmatism, in its literal sense, was very much the American philosophy of life. Pragmatism, in the philosophic sense adopted by Dewey, fit perfectly onto such a foundation. It was as if they were made for each other. It is doubtful whether such a philosophy could have grown anywhere else. The complementary positivism which came to the fore in Europe (especially in Vienna) around the same time was neither so adaptable nor so practical in the everyday sense. Where European positivism adapted itself to science, pragmatism saw itself as science in action.

Only now, at the outset of the twenty-first century, can we begin to detect a drift away from the use of such thinking. Science has now become highly abstruse and technical. It is both abstract and specialized far beyond the reach of our common understanding. Most of us cannot begin to comprehend, let alone apply, its general techniques. Science's most profound recent theories rely not at all upon experimental technique. The Big Bang and the minutest superstrings are constructs of theory upon theory. Even the certainties of hard science have begun to crumble. Scientific laws are increasingly seen as probabilitistic. Complexity and chaos theory are leading us toward a *different* science. The latest techniques and theories can no longer be given fruitful application in subjects ranging from psychology to social planning. Analogies from quantum theory, for instance, have largely proved disastrous, revealing only pretentious ignorance in those who attempt to apply them.

Dewey's philosophy served its time better than most. It also led humanity astray less than most. (One only has to compare pragmatism to other, better-known twentieth-century isms.) Dewey, an evidently decent and publicly concerned man, would probably regard such faint praise as an accolade. Had he been alive today, he would doubtless have been working upon the flexibility of his intrumentalism, adapting it as far as possible to the real requirements of the real world. He was always the first to recognize that new instruments are required for a new age.

From Dewey's Writings

The opinion which is fated to be ultimately agreed to by all who investigate is what we mean by truth, and the object represented by this opinion is the real.

> —C. S. Peirce, stating the core belief of pragmatism

If the term "matter" is given a philosophic interpretation, over and above its technical scientific meaning—e.g., *mass* until recently—this meaning, I believe, should be to name a *functional* relation rather than a substance.

> —John Dewey, *Experience, Knowledge and Value*

Character is the interpenetration of habits.
—John Dewey, *Human Nature and Conduct*

To assume that anything can be known in isolation from its connections with other things is to identify knowing with merely having some object before perception or in feeling, and is thus to lose the key to the traits that distinguish an object as known. . . . The more connections and interactions we ascertain, the more we *know* the object in question.
—John Dewey, *The Later Works 1925–1953*

Values are values, things immediately having certain intrinsic qualities. Of them as values there is accordingly nothing to be said; they are what they are. All that can be said of them concerns their generative conditions and the consequences to which they give rise. The notion that things as direct values lend themselves to thought and discourse rests upon a confusion of causal categories with immediate qualities. Objects, for example, may be distinguished as contributory or as fulfilling, but this is distinction of place with respect to causal relationship; it is not a distinction of values. We may be interested in a thing, be concerned with it or like it, for a reason. The reason for appreciation, for an enjoyed appropriation, is often that the object in question serves as a means to something; or the reason is that it stands as the culmination of an antecedent process. . . . Things that are means and things that are fulfillments have different qualities.

—John Dewey, *The Structure of Experience*

Good things change and vanish not only with changes in the environing medium but with changes in ourselves. Continued perception, except when it has been cultivated through prior criticism, dulls itself; it is soon satiated, exhausted, blasé. The infinite flippancy of the natural man is a standing theme for discourse by shrewd observers of human nature. Cultivated taste alone is capable of prolonged appreciation of the same object; and it is capable of it because it has been trained to a discriminating procedure which constantly uncovers in the object new meanings to be perceived and enjoyed.

—John Dewey, *The Structure of Experience*

. . . The whole history of science, art, and morals proves that the mind that appears *in* individuals is not as such individual mind. The former is in itself a system of belief, recognitions, and ignorances, of acceptances and rejections, of expectancies and appraisals of meanings which have been instituted under the influence of custom and tradition.

—John Dewey, *The Later Works, 1925–1953*

. . . Psychology, supplying us with knowledge of the behavior of experience, is a conception of democracy. Its postulate is that since experience fulfills itself in individuals, since it administers itself through their instrumentality, the account of the course and method of this achievement is a significant and indispensable affair.

Democracy is possible only because of a change in intellectual conditions. It implies tools for getting at truth in detail, and day by day, as we go along. Only such possession justifies the surrender of fixed, all-embracing principles to which, as universals, all particulars and individuals are subject for valuation and regulation. Without such possession, it is only the courage of the fool that would undertake the venture to which democracy has committed itself—the ordering of life in response to the needs of the moment in accordance with the ascertained truth of the moment. Modern life involves the deification of the here and now; of the specific, the particular, the unique, that which happens once and has no measure of value save such as it brings with itself. Such deification is monstrous fetishism, unless the deity be there; unless the universal lives, moves, and has its being in experience as individualized.

—John Dewey, *The Structure of Experience*

Finally, in connection with the relation of philosophy and culture, we may felicitate ourselves that we live where free discussion and free criticism are still values which are not denied us by some power reaching out for a monopoly of cultural and spiritual life. The inability of human beings in so many parts of the world to engage in free exchange of ideas should make us aware, by force of contrast, of the privilege we still enjoy and of our duty of defending and extending it. It should make us aware that free thought itself, free inquiry, is crippled and finally paralyzed by suppression of free communication. Such communication includes the right and responsibility of submitting every idea and belief to severest criticism. It is less important that we all believe alike than that we all inquire freely and put at the disposal of one another such glimpses as we may obtain of the truth for which we are in search.

—John Dewey, *Experience, Knowledge and Value*

Chronology of Significant Philosophical Dates

6th C B.C.	The beginning of Western philosophy with Thales of Miletus.
End of 6th C B.C.	Death of Pythagoras.
399 B.C.	Socrates sentenced to death in Athens.
c 387 B.C.	Plato founds the Academy in Athens, the first university.
335 B.C.	Aristotle founds the Lyceum in Athens, a rival school to the Academy.

324 A.D.	Emperor Constantine moves capital of Roman Empire to Byzantium.
400 A.D.	St. Augustine writes his *Confessions*. Philosophy absorbed into Christian theology.
410 A.D.	Sack of Rome by Visigoths heralds opening of Dark Ages.
529 A.D.	Closure of Academy in Athens by Emperor Justinian marks end of Hellenic thought.
Mid-13th C	Thomas Aquinas writes his commentaries on Aristotle. Era of Scholasticism.
1453	Fall of Byzantium to Turks, end of Byzantine Empire.
1492	Columbus reaches America. Renaissance in Florence and revival of interest in Greek learning.
1543	Copernicus publishes *On the Revolution of the Celestial Orbs*, proving mathematically that the earth revolves around the sun.

1633	Galileo forced by church to recant heliocentric theory of the universe.
1641	Descartes publishes his *Meditations*, the start of modern philosophy.
1677	Death of Spinoza allows publication of his *Ethics*.
1687	Newton publishes *Principia*, introducing concept of gravity.
1689	Locke publishes *Essay Concerning Human Understanding*. Start of empiricism.
1710	Berkeley publishes *Principles of Human Knowledge*, advancing empiricism to new extremes.
1716	Death of Leibniz.
1739–1740	Hume publishes *Treatise of Human Nature*, taking empiricism to its logical limits.
1781	Kant, awakened from his "dogmatic slumbers" by Hume, publishes *Critique of Pure Reason*.

Great era of German metaphysics begins.

1807 Hegel publishes *The Phenomenology of Mind*, high point of German metaphysics.

1818 Schopenhauer publishes *The World as Will and Representation*, introducing Indian philosophy into German metaphysics.

1889 Nietzsche, having declared "God is dead," succumbs to madness in Turin.

1921 Wittgenstein publishes *Tractatus Logico-Philosophicus*, claiming the "final solution" to the problems of philosophy.

1920s Vienna Circle propounds Logical Positivism.

1927 Heidegger publishes *Being and Time*, heralding split between analytical and Continental philosophy.

1943 Sartre publishes *Being and Nothingness*, advancing

Heidegger's thought and instigating existentialism.

1953   Posthumous publication of Wittgenstein's *Philosophical Investigations*. High era of linguistic analysis.

Chronology of Dewey's Life and Times

1859	John Dewey born in Burlington, Vermont, on October 20.
1861	Outbreak of the American Civil War. Father volunteers for Union army. Family moves to Virginia to be near father.
1865	Dewey family returns to Burlington at end of Civil War.
1879	Graduates from University of Vermont.
1879	Becomes high school teacher in Oil City, Pennsylvania.

1882	Renews studies at the Johns Hopkins University in Baltimore.
1884	Awarded Ph.D., begins teaching at the University of Michigan.
1886	Marries Alice Chipman.
1887	Publishes his first book, *Psychology*, which causes controversy.
1894	Takes a position at the newly founded University of Chicago.
1902	Publishes *The Child and the Curriculum*, outlining later version of his philosophy of education.
1904	Resigns post at Chicago after disagreements with President William Rainey Harper; takes new position at Columbia University in New York.
1914–1918	World War I.
1916	Publishes *Democracy and Education*.
1919	Visits Japan.

1920–1921	Spends academic year in China.
1927	Wife Alice dies.
1928	Visits Soviet Russia.
1937	Heads commission in Mexico City to interview Trotsky.
1938	Publishes *Logic, the Theory of Inquiry*.
1939–1945	World War II.
1946	Marries Roberta Grant at the age of eighty-seven.
1949	Dewey's ninetieth birthday celebrations spark worldwide interest.
1952	Dies in New York at the age of ninety-two.

Recommended Reading

Joseph Brent, *Charles Sanders Peirce: A Life* (Indiana University Press, 1998). The tragic life and ideas of the man whose ideas would belatedly play such a leading role in Dewey's version of pragmatism. A great but unjustly neglected American philosopher.

John Dewey, *Logic, the Theory of Inquiry*, Jo A. Boydston, ed. (Southern Illinois University Press, 1991). Dewey's central work, in which he established the ideas that lay at the heart of his philosophy and thus played a guiding role in all his other psychological, educational, and social thinking.

John Dewey, *The Quest for Certainty* (Putnam,

1960). A good introduction to Dewey's philosophy and how it relates to all his other concerns.

George Dykhuizen, *The Life and Mind of John Dewey* (Southern Illinois University Press, 1974). Surprisingly, this is one of the few full-length biographies of Dewey. It covers all the main details of his life and provides an outline of his ideas over a wide field. It is particularly good at quoting relevant sources.

Steven C. Rockefeller, *John Dewey: Religious Faith and Democratic Humanism* (Columbia University Press, 1991). An exhaustive, six-hundred-plus-page examination of Dewey's ideas in relation to his life and times.

Paul Arthur Schilpp and Lewis Edwin Hahn, eds., *The Philosophy of John Dewey* (Open Court, 1989). A comprehensive series of essays and commentaries on Dewey. Also included is a biographical essay and passages from Dewey's responses to his critics.

Index

A NOTE ON THE AUTHOR

Paul Strathern has lectured in philosophy and mathematics and now lives and writes in London. A Somerset Maugham prize winner, he is also the author of books on history and travel as well as five novels. His articles have appeared in a great many publications, including the *Observer* (London) and the *Irish Times*. His own degree in philosophy was earned at Trinity College, Dublin.

Thomas Aquinas in 90 Minutes
Aristotle in 90 Minutes
St. Augustine in 90 Minutes
Berkeley in 90 Minutes
Confucius in 90 Minutes
Derrida in 90 Minutes
Descartes in 90 Minutes
Dewey in 90 Minutes
Foucault in 90 Minutes
Hegel in 90 Minutes
Heidegger in 90 Minutes
Hume in 90 Minutes
Kant in 90 Minutes
Kierkegaard in 90 Minutes
Leibniz in 90 Minutes
Locke in 90 Minutes
Machiavelli in 90 Minutes
Marx in 90 Minutes
J. S. Mill in 90 Minutes
Nietzsche in 90 Minutes
Plato in 90 Minutes
Rousseau in 90 Minutes
Bertrand Russell in 90 Minutes
Sartre in 90 Minutes
Schopenhauer in 90 Minutes
Socrates in 90 Minutes
Spinoza in 90 Minutes
Wittgenstein in 90 Minutes